days

TO WALKING
WITH GOD
IN THE
WORKPLACE

R. LARRY MOYER

*R. Lary Moyer
John 5:24*

Kregel
Publications

*To those believers in the workplace whose
goal is to make an eternal impact on the
people with whom they work.*

31 Days to Walking with God in the Workplace

© 2010 by Evantell, Inc.

Published by Kregel Publications, a division of Kregel, Inc.,
P.O. Box 2607, Grand Rapids, MI 49501.

Library of Congress Cataloging-in-Publication Data
Moyer, R. Larry (Richard Larry)
    31 days to walking with God in the workplace / R. Larry
Moyer.
       p. cm.
1. Employees—Prayers and devotions. 2. Work—
Religious aspects—Christianity—Meditations. I. Title.
BV4593.M69   2010   242'.88—dc22   2009046877

ISBN 978-0-8254-3568-3

Printed in the United States of America

10 11 12 13 14 / 5 4 3 2 1

You Are in Full-time Ministry

To Read

> *Then the Lord spoke to Moses, saying: "See, I have called by name Bezalel the son of Uri, the son of Hur, of the tribe of Judah. And I have filled him with the Spirit of God, in wisdom, in understanding, in knowledge, and in all manner of workmanship."*
>
> —Exodus 31:1–3

To Consider

Ask the average believer, "Do you know anyone who is in full-time ministry?" He usually will mention a pastor, youth director, women's ministry director, Christian school administrator, a professor at a Bible college, or maybe a missionary. Even though these are good answers, these people make up the minority.

The *majority* of full-time Christian workers are in the *secular* workplace. That's right! As a committed believer, if you are serving the Lord as a contractor, secretary, insurance salesman, hair stylist, teacher, realtor, gymnastics instructor, engineer, CEO of a corporation, manager of a department store, or in any other occupation, you are in full-time Christian service. The only difference between you and an employee of a church is the source of your respective incomes.

Bezalel is an excellent biblical example of a person who was in full-time ministry in the workplace. His name means, "in the shadow of God." What a fitting description for a man who followed God in all he did, especially in his work. Note that Bezalel was a workplace leader, not a preacher, and yet he was filled with the Spirit of God.

His God-given ability to work with precious metals, masonry, and woodwork was widely recognized by his peers. But beyond his craftsmanship, Bezalel was a man of godly character. God chose him to be the principal designer and chief builder of the holy tabernacle. The phrase translated here as "I have called" also means "I have specially designated, appointed, and set apart Bezalel to superintend this work." Bezalel was in full-time ministry.

Congratulations! As a committed believer in your workplace, you are called to be in full-time ministry. Just as someone is "ordained" to be a pastor or youth director, you have been chosen by God to labor in your place of work. Your high and noble calling is not to be taken lightly, because you have the opportunity to impact people whom full-time employees of a church or religious association may never reach. Enjoy the work God has placed before you.

To Illustrate

R. Wilfred Grenfell, a medical missionary to Labrador, was a guest at a dinner in London. A number of socially prominent British men and women were also in attendance. During the dinner, the woman next to Wilfred Grenfell turned to him and said, "Is it true, Dr. Grenfell, that you are a missionary?" Dr. Grenfell replied, "Is it true, Madam, that you are not?"

All committed believers should see themselves in full-time Christian service, regardless of where or how they serve.

To Meditate

As you contemplate each day, do you see another day of work or another day of ministry?

To Pray

Ask God to help you see yourself each day as a missionary going to *your* mission field—the secular workplace.

Day 2

Which One Are You?

To Read

> When He saw the multitudes, He was moved with
> compassion for them, because they were weary and
> scattered, like sheep having no shepherd. Then He said
> to His disciples, "The harvest truly is plentiful, but the
> laborers are few. Therefore pray the Lord of the harvest
> to send out laborers into His harvest."
>
> —Matthew 9:36–38

To Consider

Two kinds of Christians enter the workplace every
Monday morning: One says, "I am a Christian, called to
serve the Lord as an engineer." The other says, "I'm an
engineer who happens to be a Christian." The first sees
the workplace as his calling. The second sees his faith and
his work as a coincidence. The first sees the workplace as
a ministry. The second sees the workplace as just a job.

Scripture constantly records Jesus Christ being moved
with compassion toward the lost. To reach them, He sent
out the disciples two by two, calling them "laborers" who
would reap a harvest of souls. But the disciples weren't
nearly enough; Jesus said, "The harvest truly is great, but
the laborers are few," (Luke 10:2).

The harvest is plentiful. Too often we see "the lost" as

people in deepest Africa. But the lost also live in our city, on our street, they work with us. They are construction workers, plumbers, nurses, schoolteachers, politicians, veterinarians, store clerks, and waiters. The list is almost endless. Maybe the person sitting in the desk right next to you doesn't know Jesus. The world is filled with people who need the gospel, many of whom are ripe for harvest!

Our "field of harvest" is the place where we work. God has sent us to our specific jobs to be laborers for His kingdom. As the job meets our physical needs for income, experience, and so on, we can meet the spiritual needs our coworkers may not even know they have. As you go forth to work in His field, pray that He will send laborers to work with you and that He will send an abundant harvest. You're not a worker who happens to be a Christian; you're a Christian God has assigned to your workplace.

To Illustrate

Alice Lee Humphries, in her book *Angels in Pinafores*, tells of an experience she had as a first-grade teacher. A girl came to school one day wearing a beautiful white angora beret, white mittens, and a matching muff. A mischievous little boy grabbed the white muff and threw it into the mud. After disciplining the boy, Alice comforted the girl. Brushing the mud off of the muff, the little girl looked at her teacher and said, "Sometime I must take a day off and tell him about God."

The harvest is plentiful. Whether it be in a school system, factory, or business complex, God has placed you where you are in order to impact others for Christ. They need to know Him.

To Meditate

As you enter the door at work, do you view yourself as God's laborer and your workplace as His field? Why, or why not?

To Pray

Ask God to use you as a laborer to present the gospel to a lost person at work. Then ask Him to send additional believers who will labor with you in pursuit of His harvest.

Day 3

If You Believe It, Live It!

To Read

Exhort bondservants to be obedient to their own masters, to be well pleasing in all things, not answering back, not pilfering, but showing all good fidelity, that they may adorn the doctrine of God our Savior in all things.
—Titus 2:9–10

To Consider

Your life is under a microscope. Believing as you do, it is important to live as you should—not because you need to "earn points" with God or to work your way into heaven (eternal life is a free gift that cannot be earned), but because God has called you to reflect the light of the gospel in your life.

Paul is teaching within the context of slaves and their masters, a common workplace situation in his day. But his words apply to our lives as well, in the context of employees and employers. The worker is to obey the employer. When Paul writes, "in all things," he assumes that the employer is not asking the employee to do something that contradicts Scripture. (However, if you find yourself in this type of situation, respond by seeking wise counsel and acting with integrity.)

As employees, your conduct before your employer

needs to be consistently obedient. Both your attitude and your actions matter. "Answering back" reveals a grumbling attitude that is not pleasing to God. We all struggle in this area. But no matter what provocation might exist, an employee cannot say one thing to his employer's face and another thing behind her back. Paul exhorts the slave to please the master in every way. The same applies to employees and employers.

Paul also mentioned "pilfering," or stealing. When the master's back was turned, petty larceny often was committed. "My master owes me this" was an excuse slaves often used. Sound familiar? Instead, Paul encouraged slaves to show "all good fidelity." In the same way, as employees we need to be completely trustworthy. Keep in mind that "pilfering" applies to everything from money to office supplies to *time*. Statistics show that employees waste an average of twenty percent of every workday surfing the Internet or writing and answering e-mails, outside of the jobs or tasks they are being paid to do.

As we work, we have the opportunity to "adorn the doctrine of God our Savior in all things." So live in such a way that those around you are forced to say, "If Jesus did this for you, He must be wonderful. I'd like to have what you have in my life." To that end, live out what you believe.

To Illustrate

Pulpit Helps told the story of a worldly, godless man who came to Christ. When he was asked what one thing was responsible for his conversion, he answered, "The example of one of my clerks." He explained, "This young man was one whose religion was in his life rather than his tongue. He did not bless God and speak evil of his fellow man. In fact, this man, though he never spoke a word to me on the subject of religion, exercised an influence for good over me wielded by no other human being. To him, under God, I am indebted more than to any other, for the hope in which I now rejoice of eternal life though our Lord Jesus Christ."

To Meditate

God wants to use you to change people's lives, but it's difficult to make a difference *if you aren't different*.

To Pray

Ask God to help you to consistently model Christ both in your actions and reactions to all those you encounter in your workplace.

Day 4

Are You Scared to Witness in the Workplace?

To Read

*[Pray] always with all prayer and supplication in the
Spirit, being watchful to this end with all perseverance
and supplication for all the saints—and for me, that utterance may be given to me, that I may open my mouth
boldly to make known the mystery of the gospel, for
which I am an ambassador in chains; that in it I may
speak boldly, as I ought to speak.*

—Ephesians 6:18–20

To Consider

It's your turn. Jesus Christ found you years ago. You
may have met Him through a friend who shared the
gospel with you. Now you have the same kind of opportunity. But are your knees knocking, lips quivering,
and palms sweating at the thought?

We all feel that way at times. But the solution is simple.
Pray. In fact, ask others to pray with you and for you as
you seek to share the gospel.

The apostle Paul wanted to speak loudly and consistently the "mystery of the gospel." He wanted to spread
the great message that through Jesus' work on the cross,
Gentiles and Jews are one in the body of Christ. The

12

Romans considered Christians to be a sect of the Jews. Jews considered Christians to be a bunch of heretics. So Paul's message was not a popular one. Had he spoken about general religious things or philosophies, he probably would have made friends instead of enemies. When he preached the gospel, he immediately made enemies instead of friends.

So he asked his brothers and sisters in Christ to pray for two things. First, he asked them to pray "that utterance may be given to me." Literally, he was saying, "Pray that when I open my mouth, something will come out of it." The second thing he asked them to pray for was boldness, "that I may open my mouth boldly."

We all need to cultivate brothers and sisters in Christ who will regularly pray for us—and vice versa. After all, we are His messengers to the workplace. Regularly, we all need to ask God that when we open our mouths to speak something will come out of them and that what comes out will come out *boldly*. Ask and, because God answers prayer, we will experience boldness that overtakes fear instead of fear that overtakes boldness.

To Illustrate

While accompanying me on a speaking engagement to Billings, Montana, my wife, Tammy, found herself sitting next to a man who was "religious" but did not know the Lord. As they discussed the beauty of the Montana mountains, Tammy turned the conversation from the creation to the Creator to Christ. After she explained the gospel, he promised her that *that day* he would get alone with God and trust Jesus as Savior. My wife often confesses to being fearful when it comes to evangelism. But that day, she was able to speak boldly, because she had asked many close to her to pray regularly that she would have utterance and boldness in sharing the gospel.

To Meditate

As you prepare to speak to the lost, have you also prepared by asking believers to speak to God about you?

To Pray

Ask God for brothers and sisters who will commit themselves to praying regularly for your boldness in the workplace. Then ask God to answer their prayers by giving you both utterance and boldness in evangelism.

Day 5

Live for People, Not for Things

To Read

> *For what is our hope, or joy, or crown of rejoicing? Is it*
> *not even you in the presence of our Lord Jesus Christ at*
> *His coming? For you are our glory and joy.*
> —1 Thessalonians 2:19–20

To Consider

Take five minutes. Find a quiet place. Bedroom.
Kitchen. Garage. Beneath a tree in the backyard. The
corner of a porch.

Close your eyes and imagine that you are in heaven,
face to face with Jesus. Will you be excited about the way
you've spent your life, the way you've honored Him with
your priorities and your choices? Or will you wish that
you had done things differently? What will you wish had
been the most important things in your life?

The apostle Paul was proud, but of the right things—
his new converts, the people he had led to Jesus Christ
over the years. So he asked the question, "For what is our
hope, or joy, or crown of rejoicing?"

Paul's rephrasing of the question actually answers itself.
He exclaimed, "Is it not even you in the presence of our
Lord Jesus Christ at His coming? For *you* are our glory

and joy." Paul would receive his reward at the Lord's return because he had invested his life in people.

Examine your workplace. Are you conscious that God wants to use you—directly or indirectly—to bring people to Christ? A kind word or thoughtful gesture might lead to an opportunity to share your personal testimony over lunch. A friendship may give you an opportunity to invite a coworker to a special service at your church. Walking alongside someone in a time of grief may provide the opportunity to tell of God's love as expressed through His Son. And don't forget about your retirement years. God may allow you to give even more time to people—time that you did not have when you were working full-time.

Your workplace is full of opportunities to impact people for eternity. Remember, we are called to live for people, not for things. Things are temporary, but people are eternal. And one day, when those who were saved through your witness stand before the Lord, you will be able to say, "You are my glory and joy."

To Illustrate

The Los Angeles Dodgers once played several exhibition games in Japan. Before the games, one of the host cities presented Dodgers' superstar pitcher Sandy Koufax with a bouquet of flowers. They chose a city official's granddaughter to present the flowers to Koufax. She said, "These flowers will die, Koufax-san, but you will smell forever."

People last; things don't.

To Meditate

As you examine your priorities and values, are people more important to you than things? Do your actions match your priorities?

To Pray

Ask God to make people important in your life, so much so that it becomes obvious in the way you prioritize your schedule from month to month.

Day 6

Would You Hire Yourself?

To Read

> *Therefore, whatever you want men to do to you, do also to them, for this is the Law and the Prophets.*
> —Matthew 7:12

To Consider

Line up ten employers. Ask them each the same question: "What is the biggest frustration you face in the workplace?"

Most likely, they will all give the same answer: "It's hard to find people who are willing to work. People want the pay and the benefits, but they don't want to do the work."

Matthew 7:12 is probably one of the best-known verses in the Bible. It is commonly called the "Golden Rule," and in it Christ summarized the teachings from His Sermon on the Mount (Matt. 5–7). The principle He established was simple. We need to treat others in the way that we would want to be treated. In other words, we demonstrate His righteousness in our actions.

Why is it that so many of us apply that verse everywhere but in the workplace? If you want to hire good workers, you need to be sure that you are a competent, hard worker. If you want your employer to treat you fairly and reward your hard work appropriately, you need to be the kind of worker that merits that type of response.

Ask yourself, "Am I the kind of worker I would hire?" Are you self-motivated, or does the boss need to prod you to meet deadlines? Do you consistently come to work late and overextend your lunch break? Is your work sloppy? Do you waste your employer's resources? Does your unnecessary chatter prevent others from doing their work? Do you take two hours to do a particular project when—with a bit more diligence—it could be completed in one? Do you falsify reports? Does your attitude change when performing a task you don't enjoy? Are you willing to stay late when the workload demands it?

Do you think your employer is glad he or she hired you?

To Illustrate

Reader's Digest once told of a seventy-year-old woman who called a furnace repairman. After a quick inspection, the repairman put oil into the motor and then handed her a bill for $70.00 with the description marked, "labor charges." The woman exclaimed, "But it only took you five minutes!" The repairman explained that his company had a minimum one-hour charge for every house call. The woman demanded, "Then I want my remaining fifty-five minutes of labor." She handed him a rake, and he spent the next fifty-five minutes raking leaves in her backyard.

The practice of requiring a minimum charge is proper in most cases, but the illustration serves a purpose. We ought to ask ourselves, "Am I charging my employer for an hour's work and working less than that?"

To Meditate

When you go to work, do you do all you can or simply all you must?

To Pray

Ask God to help you to be such a good worker that your work ethic serves as a testimony to Christ and as an example to others.

Day 7

Trust God! He Knows It All!

To Read

> *Commit your way to the LORD,*
> *Trust also in Him,*
> *And He shall bring it to pass.*
> *He shall bring forth your righteousness as the light,*
> *And your justice as the noonday.*
> —Psalm 37:5–6

To Consider

The good work you do is constantly overlooked. Someone was promoted ahead of you, but you know that the way he landed the promotion was deceitful. Your supervisor notices every mistake you make and even rants about them publicly. But rarely does he applaud your accomplishments. You know that the company would not be where it is today without you. However, that fact never seems to be taken into consideration—especially when it comes to a significant pay raise, recognition at an end-of-the-year company banquet, or even an "employee of the month" award. The number of years you have proven yourself to be a dependable, trustworthy employee seems of little importance. Yet you enjoy what you do and don't like the thought of walking away from it.

The truth of Psalm 37:5–6 should lift your spirit and keep you on track. "Commit" means to roll the burden of your life's cares upon the Lord. The Hebrew word used here portrays a man who takes a burden far too heavy for him to carry by himself and rolls it upon the shoulders of one who is more capable of bearing it. The psalmist adds in verse 5, "and He shall bring it to pass." The idea is that God will handle anything that concerns you. He will take care of any anxiety you have about whether you will go as far up the career ladder as you need to or make as much money as you need to make. Placed in His hands, the ultimate outcome of your life in the workplace will never be disappointing.

Verse 6 continues, "He shall bring forth your righteousness as the light, and your justice as the noonday." Simply put, any good you have done will be as noticeable as the brilliant light of the sun in the middle of the day. Every one of your good works will be noticed, no matter how small they might seem to others. If you have suffered unjustly, God will point His finger at those who pointed at you. He will be your defense attorney, and any declaration He makes about you will be final and flawless.

In other words, He is the one who does your performance evaluation. Any good that has gone unnoticed by others has been noted by Him. Any unfairness you have suffered will be obvious when God's righteousness and justice prevail. Someone else's evaluation of you may have left a lot to be desired, but God knows it all. Trust Him!

To Illustrate

D. L. Moody is reported to have said, "Trust in yourself, and you are doomed to disappointment. Trust in your money, and you may have it taken from you. Trust in your friends, and they will die and leave you. But trust in God, and you will never be confounded in time or eternity."

To Meditate

When difficult situations or uncertainties occur at work, do you respond with faith or fretting?

To Pray

Ask God to give you a calm heart and mind at work that results from an upward look to Him rather than a horizontal look at others.

Day 8

He Is Your Supervisor

To Read

> *Masters, do the same things to them, giving up threaten-*
> *ing, knowing that your own Master also is in heaven,*
> *and there is no partiality with Him.*
>
> —Ephesians 6:9

To Consider

Supervisors and managers are generally responsible for overseeing their employees, directing their work, and evaluating their performance. But supervisors also must recognize that just as some employees report to them, they also report to someone else. That "someone else" is Jesus Christ.

In Ephesians 6, the apostle Paul was speaking to masters and slaves—the labor situation that existed in Paul's day. But his teaching is just as applicable for today's employers and employees.

The master's mode of operation was often the use of threats. If certain conditions were not met, consequences would follow. A proverbial expression of the time said that "all slaves are enemies." Hence, masters often were abusive tyrants. Their manner of abuse ranged from the sexual harassment of female slaves to threats to sell slaves away from their families, from physical beatings to death in the Roman arena. Too often, slaves didn't serve their masters out of respect; they served out of fear. Paul says, "Stop threatening your people!"

Instead, Paul commanded masters to treat their slaves with integrity and goodwill. Just as slaves were accountable to them, masters were accountable to God. And God shows no partiality. With Him there is no favoritism. He expects obedience from slaves and masters alike.

The application to Christian employers is obvious. You are accountable to God for your attitudes, words, and actions toward your employees. You, too, have a Master. The way you conduct yourselves toward and around your employees should be honoring to God. What you permit in the workplace is a critical issue. Sexual harassment, unlawful behavior, and unethical dealings cannot be tolerated and must be dealt with quickly.

As a Christian, you will one day stand before Christ to be rewarded. Just as your employees have been the objects of your evaluation, you will be the object of His. After all, you report to Him. Your evaluation of others might be flawed; His evaluation of you will be flawless. He will not have to go to someone else to get the facts; He already knows them. Even a CEO ultimately answers to more than stockholders or a board of directors. One day, he or she will stand face to face with the Savior.

To Illustrate

In his book *Be Rich*, Warren Wiersbe tells of a friend of his who was promoted to a place of executive leadership. Unfortunately, it filled him with so much pride that he not only enjoyed the new privileges, but he also was quick to let his employees know who was in charge. He eventually lost the respect of his workers. Their productivity decreased so badly that the board of directors had to replace him.

Wiersbe concluded, "Because my friend forgot that he had a 'Master in heaven,' he failed to be a good 'master on earth.'"

To Meditate

If today were the day of your performance evaluation from your ultimate Supervisor, how would you measure up?

To Pray

Ask God to help you to supervise others with integrity, honoring *your* Master.

Day 9

Are You Asking God for Opportunities?

To Read

> *[Pray] also for us, that God would open to us a door for the word, to speak the mystery of Christ, for which I am also in chains.*
>
> —Colossians 4:3

To Consider

You *want* to talk to a person at work about Christ, but you just haven't found the right opportunity. Correction. You want to talk with many people about Christ, but the opportunities just don't seem to present themselves.

Have you asked God to open doors for you to share the gospel?

When Paul wrote to the Colossians, he was a prisoner of the Roman Empire, most likely chained to a Roman soldier twenty-four hours a day. No doubt Paul had the opportunity to share Christ in prison. At the same time, Paul and his coworkers, Timothy and Epaphras, were limited by the nature of their situation. So he asked fellow believers to pray "that God would open to us a door for the word." He requested prayer for *opportunity*.

Opportunities for evangelism on the job come in numerous ways. They are as varied as the workplace itself. A coworker might come in one morning, trembling with the news that his wife has just been diagnosed with cancer. Your offer to pray for him may result in a future opportunity to share the gospel with him. A woman may confide in you that she has discovered her husband is having an affair. An offer to talk after work may give you the opportunity to comfort her, explaining that the One who instituted marriage is also the One who can make it work. Forgiveness extended to a person who misrepresented you may cause her to ask, "What makes you so different?" Volunteering a ride to work one morning—particularly one that takes you considerably out of your way—may be a great way to let others know that you care. Acts of kindness like these may allow you the opportunity to share a tract that talks about the One who cared for us even to the point of dying for us.

God will open doors for you to share the gospel. But are you asking Him to do so? And are you willing to put forth the effort and respond?

To Illustrate

A policeman I know trains as many as thirty officers at a time in tactical deployment issues such as those relating to mass shootings. He consistently has the opportunity to tell those he trains, "The thing we must remember about what we do is that when we leave in the morning, there is no certainty we will come home. Although that is true of any profession, that is particularly true of us because of the danger we face. But even though you cannot be certain you'll come home to a house on earth, you can be certain you will go to heaven." Then he shares his testimony.

What an opportunity—God has opened a door for my friend to share the gospel out of the work he does every single day.

To Meditate

Reflect on the unlimited power of God. Our God is so powerful that He can open a door today that was closed just yesterday.

To Pray

Ask God to give you an opportunity this week to share the gospel with a coworker, and then grasp the opportunity when it comes.

Day 10

Are You Mastered by Money?

To Read

> *No one can serve two masters; for either he will hate the one and love the other, or else he will be loyal to the one and despise the other. You cannot serve God and mammon.*

—Matthew 6:24

To Consider

Money. Cars. Houses. Hobbies. Clothing. Vacations.

Now, here's the question. Which one of these six things stands the greatest chance of becoming your master?

The answer is obvious, isn't it? Money. The reason is just as obvious. Money is the means and driving force behind the others. Money obtains a newer and better car for us, provides us with a bigger home, allows us to indulge in our hobbies, enables us to expand our wardrobe, and lets us choose our next exotic vacation destination. If the money is there, virtually no material things are beyond our reach. There is nothing inherently wrong with that—unless we come to a point where money controls us, taking the place of our other priorities and values.

Christ's warning to His disciples was most appropriate. No one can serve two masters. Sooner or later they will make opposing demands. He does not want us, as His disciples, to divide our allegiance to Him with anyone or anything.

"Mammon" refers to wealth, money, or property—anything material in nature. None of those things are wrong in and of themselves. In fact, if they are properly used, they can have eternal dividends. Money given toward a short-term mission trip can result in a harvest of people coming to Christ. Property used for an outreach retreat can lead to non-Christians being impacted by the gospel. A person who volunteers his or her large backyard for a neighborhood block party can open a door for the gospel. A contribution to a single mom's housing need may see her come to Christ. Money given toward a community outreach project may result in neighbors exposed to the good news.

But what happens when we allow material things to master us? The desire for wealth will dull our moral senses as we try to call wrong "right." The love of money will prevent us from being generous and others-centered. Our focus becomes getting, not giving. More is never enough. Anxiety characterizes our lives instead of contentment. Our eyes and ears are tuned to acquisition rather than tuned to God's voice. Instead of considering everything we have as a gift from God to be used for His purposes, we abuse our blessings. Family and friends become victims of our backward priorities. Money no longer serves us; we serve it.

To Illustrate

Our Daily Bread once shared a story about a missionary who presented the gospel to a man who worshipped idols. One day the man took a small statue and coin and placed them on the table before the missionary. Then he took two slips of paper and wrote something on each one. On the note by the idol, he wrote the words "heathen god." On the sheet next to the silver coin, he wrote the words "Christian god." From what that man had observed in the lives of people from so-called Christian nations, he had concluded that money was the main object of their adoration and the source of their celebration and worship.

To Meditate

What have the monetary benefits of your workplace and paycheck become—things that serve you or things that you serve?

To Pray

Ask God to reveal any ways in which you have allowed money to become your master. Then ask Him to help you use your possessions instead of allowing them to use you.

Day 11

The Sovereignty of God as Comfort, Not Excuse

To Read

> *A man's heart plans his way,*
> *But the LORD directs his steps.*

—Proverbs 16:9

To Consider

Sometimes life doesn't go the way we want. We carefully plan our marketing strategy. We hire the right people. We analyze our proposal. We seek wise counsel. The project has "profit" and "win" written all over it. But in the end, everything falls apart. Looking back, it's hard not to feel like our time, energy, and money were wasted.

Did we do something wrong? Not necessarily. Were our motives impure? Perhaps they were the purest they've ever been. We may have even bathed the circumstances and the transaction in prayer.

In circumstances like these, we need to trust in the sovereignty of God. Planning honors the Lord. It is wise; it is what He wants and expects us to do. But in the end, He is God and we are dependent upon Him. He is never dependent upon us. In the end, He permits, overrules, or furthers our actions. He chooses what to do because He always knows best. God sees things from a perspective we cannot see. He understands things at a depth we cannot fathom. In every turn along the way, He is in complete control.

However, God's sovereignty does not excuse us from doing our part. We dare not be irresponsible or careless in our business dealings. But properly understood, the sovereignty of God is comforting. Even though we may not know *why* things do not turn out as we plan, God is sovereign, and He knows the end from the beginning.

Customer response, product development, investors, profit and loss, or injury on the job—He is aware of it all even before it occurs. We may never have the answers for why businesses fail, plans are aborted, stores close, or layoffs take place just when we think our future with the company is the brightest. But at this point, we can take comfort in one unchangeable truth: He is God! He loves us and will always move to bring about our good. He never makes mistakes. Find comfort in His sovereignty.

To Illustrate

In 1812, Napoleon and the mighty French army invaded Russia. After suffering hardship and ignominious defeat, Napoleon and his fragmented army retreated. Then they were summarily defeated by Wellington and his army at Waterloo. The would-be conqueror was exiled to a remote island for the rest of his life. In dictating his memoirs, Napoleon said, "There was a hand moving in Europe which I did not see—the hand of God."

In our personal lives, including the workplace, there is a hand moving that we often do not see—the hand of God. We can trust Him.

To Meditate

Think of two situations when things may not have gone the way you had planned—for better or for worse. Looking back, can you see God's hand in your circumstances? Thank God that He was in control and always will be.

To Pray

Ask God to help you be a responsible planner. Then ask Him to help you trust in His sovereignty, being willing to submit to His will.

Day 12

Who Is Number One?

To Read

> *Let nothing be done through selfish ambition or conceit,*
> *but in lowliness of mind let each esteem others better than*
> *himself. Let each of you look out not only for his own*
> *interests, but also for the interests of others.*
> —Philippians 2:3–4

To Consider

The word *me* is ingrained in our culture and, worse, in our minds. We have become so self-centered that making every decision to benefit ourselves is second nature. And as we spend time around self-centered people who have not met the Lord, we have to be cautious, or they will lead us instead of allowing us to lead them.

In Philippians 2:3–4, Paul pleaded with his brothers and sisters in Christ concerning how they ought to treat one another. The selfless, humble attitude he proposed also applies to our relationships with those who don't yet know the Lord Jesus. Our attitude may be the deciding factor that brings an unbeliever to Christ.

Selfish ambition and conceit should be overruled by a deep sense of humility. A humble attitude is based on valuing others above ourselves. In other words, their well-being should mean more to us than our well-being.

However, an attitude of humility does not preclude our own needs, those of our families, and those of others in the body of Christ. The last part of verse 4 explains that we are to look out "*also* for the interests of others." The point Paul is making is that we are to put other people's needs before our own. They are number one, and we are number two. Remember, Christ did not come to be served but to serve (Mark 10:45).

As you punch out at five, are you willing to be delayed—caught up in traffic—in order to give encouragement to a coworker whose mate was diagnosed with depression? Could you give some surplus funds to help a family whose expenses are about to overwhelm them? As you prepare for a father-and-son retreat, might you invite a coworker's son whose father recently died? Is there a practical plan you can implement to lighten your assistant's heavy workload? Would you leave the house half an hour early to pick up a coworker who needs a ride? When you ask a coworker about his or her weekend, are you really interested? On the "who's important" list in your life, whose name is at the top?

To Illustrate

In his book *The Man of Heroic Endurance*, Chuck Swindoll tells the story of Johnny Guenther, a college-aged young man with brain cancer. Following his very first surgery, his character and godly attitude became apparent. With his parents' approval, the surgeon went to Johnny's hospital room to explain the seriousness of his brain tumor. The boy listened attentively. Then his first question was, "Doctor, how shall we break it to my parents?"

That "others first" mentality should characterize our lives in the workplace.

To Meditate

If you were to divide up your "thinking time" into percentages, how much of it is spent on others instead of yourself? What does this tell you about your attitudes and priorities?

To Pray

Ask God to make you sensitive to areas of your life and work where you can place others before yourself.

Day 13

Never *Give Up!*

To Read

> *Therefore, my beloved brethren, be steadfast, immovable, always abounding in the work of the Lord, knowing that your labor is not in vain in the Lord.*
> —1 Corinthians 15:58

To Consider

You've tried everything you know to do—treating a coworker to lunch, sharing a compassionate word with a discouraged employer, comforting an employee going through divorce, and even sharing the good news with a person you thought was "ripe and ready" for the gospel. All of your efforts have come to nothing. Even your consistent Christian living seems to go unappreciated or unnoticed. Spiritually, it appears that nothing is happening in your workplace.

First Corinthians 15:58 gives us a needed word of encouragement, based on the fact that we serve a risen Savior. Our hope in the future ought to impact our work in the present. After expounding on the victory that is ours through the resurrection of God's Son, Paul makes a plea to every Christian.

He says, "Be steadfast, immovable, always abounding in the work of the Lord." The "work of the Lord" need not be restricted. It can include everything from our own spiritual growth to extending help to the poor and needy. Helping a neighbor or evangelizing the lost is the Lord's work. Living a pure life around non-Christians at work also falls into this category. Everything that you do with the motive of honoring God is His work.

We are to be steadfast and immovable, always abounding in spiritual service. "Abounding" means that our service should be like water that flows over the edges of a container—natural, real, and abundant. Such steadfastness and determination is never in vain. We'll have no regrets when we see Jesus face to face. And if we are results oriented, as many hard workers are, we can rejoice in the knowledge that we will see the results in heaven. There *is* eternal reward awaiting us (Rev. 22:12). Never give up! Never! Just keep on serving.

To Illustrate

Leadership Journal told of an incident on October 7, 1968. An hour earlier, Mamo Wolde of Ethiopia had completed a twenty-six mile marathon. As the remaining spectators prepared to leave, sirens and police whistles filled the air. John Stephen Akhwari, the last man to finish the marathon, entered the stadium. His leg bloodied and bandaged, severely injured from a fall, he grimaced with each step. In light of his injury and with no chance to win a medal, someone asked him why he chose to keep going. He replied, "My country did not send me seven thousand miles to start the race. They sent me seven thousand miles to finish it."

Even when times get tough, God wants us to *finish* well as we serve Him.

To Meditate

When you don't see results from your faithfulness in the workplace, do you look backward or upward?

To Pray

Particularly during the moments when you're discouraged with your efforts to impact the workplace, ask God to help you to keep your focus on Him rather than on the results of your efforts. Ask Him to remind you daily that anything you do for Him is not done in vain.

What Marks Your Tongue?

To Read

Let your speech always be with grace, seasoned with salt,
that you may know how you ought to answer each one.
—Colossians 4:6

To Consider

What instrument do you use most in a given workday? Here's a hint: it's not the computer, hammer, cash register, thermometer, appointment book, cell phone, white board, pen, or even your car. This instrument is a couple of inches wide, several inches long, and sits behind your teeth. Think through the number of times you use your tongue every day. Pretty incredible, isn't it?

Paul the apostle wrote to the Colossians, explaining how we are to conduct ourselves toward those who are outside of Christ. He spent a significant amount of time addressing the area of our speech. He exhorts us to always speak with *grace*. In other words, what we say should originate in the love and grace that has been given to us by God.

Next, he says that our speech should be "seasoned with salt." A well-known salt lake was situated close to ancient Colosse, so this analogy would have been very appropriate for his audience. Salt has a twofold purpose. On the one hand, it acts as a preservative, protecting perishable items from decay. On the other hand, it induces appetite by making food taste good. His point is that we ought to cultivate the discipline of pleasant and wholesome conversation, a discipline through which we may be able to cultivate in others an appetite for Jesus.

Then Paul adds, "that you may know how you ought to answer each one." Remember—God has placed you in the workplace to impact His kingdom. Perhaps your coworker has a question about God or reveals bitterness toward Him. Perhaps another has been turned off by Christians or offended by a preacher. Yet another may have a question about Christianity. You ought to speak in such a way that moves people closer to the cross, not away from it. This does not mean we can't be direct when we have to be direct. But it does mean that we have no excuse to be rude, never a reason to be harsh. Tenderness—not terseness—needs to characterize our speech.

To Illustrate

M. R. DeHaan once said, "The most deadly member in the human body is the tongue. We can kick with our feet and strike with our fist, but neither can do as much damage as a loose tongue. The bruise of a kick will heal, the black eye caused by a blow from a fist will clear up, but the wounds inflicted by unkind words, idle gossip, outright lying, and vicious slandering can never be completely healed."

As you consider the truthfulness of his words, consider the good that a gentle tongue can do—encouraging the disheartened, strengthening the fainthearted, disarming an angry person, and, most importantly, opening a door for the gospel.

To Meditate

Would your friends, family, and coworkers describe your speech as kind or cutting?

To Pray

Ask God to help you control your tongue instead of allowing your tongue to control you. Ask Him to give you speech that will open doors for the gospel.

Day 15

Redeem Your Workday

To Read

> *Walk in wisdom toward those who are outside, redeeming the time.*
>
> —Colossians 4:5

To Consider

Today. You will never have this day again. Once it is gone, it is gone. Use it; don't lose it. We need to make the most of every moment we have for the glory of God and to further His kingdom.

In Colossians 4:5, Paul explained how we ought to behave toward those who are outside—meaning outside the church and outside of Christ. We are to walk in wisdom, that is, with common, good sense, as we encounter those who don't know the Lord. And when Paul encourages us to "redeem the time," he is telling us to grasp each opportunity we have with them. We are to look at each moment of our workday as an opportunity to live around non-Christians in such a way that would draw them closer to the cross, not away from it. We are to walk in consistent Christlikeness, with our lives echoing the message we speak.

If you talk to an average non-Christian, you will probably hear the complaint, "Christians are hypocrites."

Sometimes these complaints are justified, and other times they are not. But the point is that such a complaint should never be made about us. Our daily lives at work ought to point people to the Savior. The forty hours or more we spend at work each week are opportunities to make an eternal impact on the people around us.

Such opportunities may come when others see our calmness in the midst of a personal, local, or national disaster. Our lives have maximum influence not when things are going well, but when they are going wrong. We might have a chance to "redeem the time" when we counter physical or emotional mistreatment with patience and forgiveness. We may grasp an opportunity by staying after work to help a coworker who has been ill for a week to catch up on work that is threatening to overwhelm her. A boss who knows you are a Christian might be impressed with the Savior when he witnesses your integrity in a situation in which you could have been dishonest. A fellow employee might ask, "What's different about her?" when she sees you refusing to join in gossip over lunch. Remember, you will never have *this day* again.

Redeem your workday. Make it count. Use it to honor God and to draw others nearer to Him.

To Illustrate

David Livingston was a Scottish missionary and explorer. Someone once said of him, "He never tried to convert me, but if I had been with him any longer, I would have become a Christian."

Your workplace should be a platform from which you seek to attract people to Christ. Make every day count.

To Meditate

If people were to view your life at work, would they be drawn to Jesus Christ?

To Pray

Ask God to help you be a positive witness at work through your actions and your words. Then ask Him to use your life to draw others to the Savior.

Day 16

Payback Time!

To Read

> *Repay no one evil for evil. Have regard for good things in the sight of all men. If it is possible, as much as depends on you, live peaceably with all men. Beloved, do not avenge yourselves, but rather give place to wrath; for it is written, "Vengeance is Mine, I will repay," says the Lord. Therefore*
> *"If your enemy is hungry, feed him;*
> *If he is thirsty, give him a drink;*
> *For in so doing you will heap coals of fire on his head."*
> *Do not be overcome by evil, but overcome evil with good.*
> —Romans 12:17–21

To Consider

The personnel department was underhanded and malicious. He misrepresented you to the boss. She took credit for an increase in sales that was actually your work. As a nurse, you were blamed for a mistake the doctor made. A competitor acted on a lead that he promised he'd let you pursue. Irresponsible warehouse personnel allowed you to be blamed for a problem they created.

In situations like these, the question is not about what you'd *like* to do. The answer to that is obvious. It's payback time. The real question is, what does God instruct you to do? After all, obedience to Him incurs reward; disobedience incurs a penalty (see Lev. 26).

Paul the apostle gives numerous practical instructions that apply here. Don't repay evil for evil. Your purpose on earth is not to get even. Do what is morally good or praiseworthy in the sight of men. Peace is not always within your control, but try to live peaceably with all men anyway. Your goal should be to resolve discord, not to cause it. Whatever vengeance needs to be exercised, let God do it. He is your best defense attorney. Repaying unkindness with acts of love can heap "coals of fire" on an enemy's head, causing a burning sense of shame and remorse.

All of these instructions are summarized in Paul's words, "Do not be overcome by evil, but overcome evil with good" (Rom. 12:21). "Payback time" should be used for returning good—not evil. When evil things are done to us, we do not have to strike back in revenge at the people who did those things. In fact, we can take the opportunity to do the *opposite* to them that they have done to us. Our "payback" should not be the evil they deserve but the good they don't deserve.

To Illustrate

Henry B. Fuhrman relayed a story his mother told him that greatly impacted his understanding of the proper way to pay back evil. His mother's family raised a few chickens. Frequently, they noticed the disappearance of some of the hens. And strangely enough, the next day, the neighbors always had chicken for dinner. His mother was tempted to tell the neighbors what she thought of them, but her husband had a better idea. He told her to prepare two chickens and take the delicious dish to the neighbors. She did. That was the last time any chickens disappeared.

Revenge is far less satisfying in the long run than resolution. And resolution honors God.

To Meditate

Think of two ways people at work have done you wrong. Then ask yourself, "Did I respond with the proper type of payback?"

To Pray

Ask God to consistently make you a person who pays back evil with good.

Day 17

How Balanced Are You?

To Read

*The Word became flesh and dwelt among us, and we
beheld His glory, the glory as of the only begotten of the
Father, full of grace and truth.*

—John 1:14

To Consider

We struggle with balance, don't we? Some of us lack a
good work ethic. Others are workaholics. Some neglect
family responsibilities. Others feel that family alone mat-
ters and so show little, if any, concern for a next-door
neighbor. Some never extend a helping hand. Others
wear themselves out trying to help everyone.

Lack of balance can occur in other areas too. Personal
evangelism is a terrific example. Some believers hesitate
to tell people that they are sinners, so those who are lost
fail to see their need for Christ. Others stress a person's
lost condition, but they do so in such a cold and blunt
way that non-Christians become offended.

As you evangelize in the workplace, follow Christ's
example. He was "full of grace and truth."

That balance of grace and truth is captured in John
4. Christ spoke to a woman from Samaria who was such
a social outcast that she had to come to the well at high

noon to draw water, when most people came in the evening. People did not want to be contaminated by her presence. Jesus' grace is obvious in the simple fact that He engaged in conversation with her in spite of her sinful condition. He offered her forgiveness and acceptance, saying, "If you knew the gift of God, and who it is who says to you, 'Give Me a drink,' you would have asked Him, and He would have given you living water" (v. 10).

His truth is also evident here. Jesus saw her past and her present. He remarked, "You have well said, 'I have no husband,' for you have had five husbands, and the one whom you now have is not your husband; in that you spoke truly" (John 4:17–18). Then He went on to forgive her sin, and she believed in Him.

The same balance of grace and truth should characterize your interactions with people as you evangelize your workplace. Your coworkers must understand the truth that we are all sinners who deserve to be separated from God forever. They also must see that even though they've turned their backs on Him, He has not turned His back on them. As a God of grace, He wants to give them forgiveness and favor they don't deserve. Neither grace *nor* truth alone can balance our presentation of the gospel; we need grace *and* truth.

To Illustrate

A prisoner facing execution became convicted by her sinfulness. Numerous believers walked by her cell. Their terse words and demeaning frowns conveyed the seriousness of her crime in their eyes. Finally, one believer asked for permission to talk to her. While acknowledging the horror of her sin, she shared the limitless love of God. Moments later, the prisoner trusted Christ. And as she headed toward her execution, she knew she was headed to life, not death.

God greatly used one believer to reach out with a balance of grace and truth.

To Meditate

If someone described your approach to the lost, would they characterize you as a person of grace, a person of truth, or a person of both grace *and* truth?

To Pray

Ask God to make you a person with such a balanced understanding of evangelism that you never extend truth without grace or grace without truth.

Day 18

Build Your Heavenly Bank Account

To Read

> Do not lay up for yourselves treasures on earth, where
> moth and rust destroy and where thieves break in and
> steal; but lay up for yourselves treasures in heaven,
> where neither moth nor rust destroys and where thieves
> do not break in and steal. For where your treasure is,
> there your heart will be also.
>
> —Matthew 6:19–21

To Consider

Accumulating treasures is not wrong. The Scriptures command us to do so. The issue is, what *kind* of treasures are we storing up?

What do all the following things have in common: money, cars, trucks, motorcycles, boats, clothing, diamonds, houses, trophies, sports equipment, televisions, stereos, appliances, computers, yard decorations, furniture, and expensive portraits?

Two things come to mind: they are all subject to decay, and thieves can break in and steal them. None can be labeled as "permanent." The fact that they are here today is no guarantee that they will be here tomorrow. Are you using your work and income as a means for collecting temporary things?

Suppose you were to use the workplace to lay up treasure in heaven—to build the kind of heavenly bank account that God delights in rewarding. Eternal treasure might include a favor done for a coworker, a kind response to an insulting remark, a deed that places someone else's well-being before your own, encouragement for a coworker whose sibling just died in a car accident, a helping hand given to a single dad, or using business profits to finance ministry. Rust or thieves cannot touch these treasures. The rewards will be eternal.

Jesus knew and understood us. Our hearts always follow our treasure, not vice versa. If earthly riches are something you treasure, your heart will be a very materialistic one. If the eternal destiny of the people you rub shoulders with each day is something you treasure, you will have a Christlike heart for lost people. If you lay up the right kind of treasure in heaven, your heart will seek after godly things. So build up your heavenly bank account. The rewards are incalculable.

To Illustrate

A British newspaper once told of a woman who had hidden $20,000 worth of jewelry in a plastic bag, hoping to prevent burglars from finding it. Later, having forgotten about it, she accidentally threw the bag out with the garbage. Workmen searched for nine hours in a landfill before finding her treasure and restoring it to her.

Two truths are obvious in this story. First, the woman's treasure was not thief-proof. Second, all the time spent searching for her treasure on earth took away time that could have been spent building up treasure in heaven.

To Meditate

Think of the "deposits" you make into your heavenly bank account while you're at work. Are the deposits increasing?

To Pray

Ask God to help you prioritize your heavenly bank account over your earthly one, recognizing and acting on the tangible things that build eternal reward.

Day 19

Something Good Out of Something Bad

To Read

Then Joseph said to his brothers, "I am Joseph; does my father still live?" But his brothers could not answer him, for they were dismayed in his presence. And Joseph said to his brothers, "Please come near to me." So they came near. Then he said: "I am Joseph your brother, whom you sold into Egypt. But now, do not therefore be grieved or angry with yourselves because you sold me here; for God sent me before you to preserve life. For these two years the famine has been in the land, and there are still five years in which there will be neither plowing nor harvesting. And God sent me before you to preserve a posterity for you in the earth, and to save your lives by a great deliverance. So now it was not you who sent me here, but God; and He has made me a father to Pharaoh, and lord of all his house, and a ruler throughout all the land of Egypt.

—Genesis 45:3–8

To Consider

"I hate my job." "The sooner I am out of here, the better." "No one could enjoy this place." Have you ever made statements like these? Your feelings may be justifiable. But have you ever imagined that something good might come out of your bad situation?

Joseph's brothers sold him as a slave. They were likely convinced he was dead. And then they discovered that he held their lives in his hands. With great fear, they had to be wondering if their brother would take his revenge.

Against all natural expectations, Joseph's response was kindness. In spite of his brothers' hateful actions, God had provided a way to preserve his father's family. Famine had devastated the land for two years and would continue for another five years. God, in His sovereignty, raised Joseph up to become second-in-command over all Egypt. Through his wise administration, Joseph preserved the lives of all those in Egypt and those of his own household. Something good came out of something evil.

Your circumstances at work may not be the best, but God always can bring something good out of something bad. He might use your consistent Christian living in the midst of adverse circumstances to impact a lost person for Christ. Maybe a relationship you build in your workplace will lead to a future opportunity for evangelism. Who knows what God has in store through layoffs, downsizing, personnel transfer, reduced hours or benefits, or departmental changes?

To Illustrate

Anyone raised around farming understands a simple principle: abundant rain on soybeans or corn crops is not always best. The plants do not have to push their roots deep in search of water. And over time, the roots remain near the surface. So when a drought comes, they are unprepared and cannot survive. However, to some degree, the absence of rain early in the season can have a positive effect by causing roots to go deeper.

As you experience drought in the workplace, remember that something good can come out of unfortunate circumstances.

To Meditate

Which do you concentrate on the most in your workplace—asking God to get you out of difficult circumstances, or trusting Him to bring about His ultimate good in your life and in the lives of others?

To Pray

Ask God to help you look for good things that can happen in adverse circumstances. Now, ask Him to help you concentrate on the good rather than the bad.

Day 20

Obedience over Opinion

To Read

> The children of Israel committed a trespass regarding the
> accursed things, for Achan the son of Carmi, the son
> of Zabdi, the son of Zerah, of the tribe of Judah, took
> of the accursed things; so the anger of the Lord burned
> against the children of Israel. . . .
>
> So the LORD said to Joshua: "Get up! Why do
> you lie thus on your face? Israel has sinned, and they
> have also transgressed My covenant which I commanded
> them. For they have even taken some of the accursed
> things, and have both stolen and deceived; and they have
> also put it among their own stuff. . . .
>
> "Get up, sanctify the people, and say, 'Sanctify
> yourselves for tomorrow, because thus says the LORD
> God of Israel: "There is an accursed thing in your midst,
> O Israel; you cannot stand before your enemies until
> you take away the accursed thing from among you."'"
>
> —Joshua 7:1, 10–11, 13

To Consider

In order to honor God in our workplace, we must
recognize that God says what He means and means what
He says.

The instructions God gave to Joshua were clear. Before

the Israelites went to conquer Jericho, He gave them a command: "All the silver and gold, and vessels of bronze and iron, are consecrated to the LORD; they shall come into the treasury of the LORD" (Josh. 6:19).

Achan didn't take God seriously; he deliberately disobeyed and kept some of the battle spoils for himself. But when Joshua and the Israelites moved on to conquer Ai, they failed miserably. Not only did they lose men, but they also were forced to retreat in the face of what should have been an easy victory (Josh. 7:1–5).

Devastated, Joshua sought the Lord. God revealed that there was disobedience within the camp. He told Joshua how to discover the guilty party and the punishment to render. Achan and his family suffered death for their disobedience. They learned the hard way that God wanted their obedience, not their opinion. God's standards could be ignored, but the consequences of disobedience couldn't be escaped.

As we go about our week, we need to ask continually for God's blessings. But we also need to be certain that sin is being handled properly. God will never ignore underhanded dealings, misrepresentations, failure to pay debts, illegal activities, falsifying reports, or impure motives. No form of evil should be tolerated (1 Thess. 5:22). Sooner or later disobedience will take its toll. God requires our obedience, not our opinion. The cost of obedience is small compared to the cost of disobedience.

To Illustrate

Our Daily Bread related the account of Sir Henry Brackenbury's life as a military attaché in Paris. In a conversation, distinguished French statesman Leon Gambretta told Brackenbury, "There are only two things a soldier needs to know. He must know how to march, and he must know how to shoot." The Englishman responded, "I beg your pardon, Excellency, but you have forgotten the most important thing of all." Gambretta asked, "What is that?" Brackenbury replied, "He must know how to obey!"

To be an effective witness for Christ in the workplace, we must know how to obey.

To Meditate

When you know what is right before God, how long do you wait or waver before you obey?

To Pray

Ask God to reveal any area of your life in the workplace that does not honor him. Pray that He will show you what you can do in your particular capacity to deal with sin and uphold righteousness.

Day 21

God Spoke Clearly.
Do You?

To Read

> *So when Jesus had received the sour wine, He said, "It is finished!" And bowing His head, He gave up His spirit.*
> —John 19:30

To Consider

The workplace is filled with opportunities for evangelism—whether during a coffee break, while enjoying lunch together, or at the close of the day as you walk to your car. Every interaction is a chance to speak the good news.

As opportunities arise, it is critical that we present the gospel *clearly*. We dare not speak confusingly when dealing with a person's eternal destiny. To speak clearly though, we must be certain we understand three simple words Christ uttered on the cross. Let me explain.

We are sinners, and because of our sin we deserve to be separated from God forever. Jesus Christ, the perfect Son of God, took our punishment for us. He was crucified in our place. He was our substitute. And on the third day, He rose from the dead, proving His victory over sin.

But note carefully Christ's declaration as He hung on the cross in our place. "It is finished!" "Finished" is the translation of the Greek word *tetelestai*. In New Testament times, receipts were stamped with the word *tetelestai,* meaning that the debts they represented had been paid in full.

On the cross, Jesus Christ did not make a "down payment" for our sins. He made the *full* payment. We are not accepted by God on the basis of Christ *plus* our good life, baptism, or religious efforts. We are accepted by God on the basis of Christ *period*. His death and resurrection verified the fact that God was completely and forever satisfied with His Son's payment for our sins. Our debt of sin was "paid in full."

Therefore, as we present the gospel, we must explain that we are sinners, that we must recognize that Christ died for us and rose from the dead, and that we must trust in Christ *alone* to save us. We must be satisfied with the thing that satisfies God. God was satisfied that His Son's death on the cross—and that alone—paid our debt of sin. Christ spoke clearly on the cross. We must echo that message just as clearly. Christ alone is our salvation.

To Illustrate

I was presenting the gospel to a non-Christian. The unbeliever explained how she tried her best to do what was right and please God. Then she said, "But, I'm not sure I've done enough. I'm afraid God will never accept me." I responded, "You're right. You haven't done enough, and you never will. God will never accept you based on *anything* you've done."

A look of astonishment appeared on the woman's face. Then I explained that God cannot accept *anything* we do as payment for our sins. But instead, God has already accepted His Son's death as full payment. And through trust in Christ alone, we can be totally right with God. Moments later, she trusted Christ.

To Meditate

Meditate on these three words: paid in full. How do they support the fact that God's gift of eternal life is truly free? In your personal presentation of the gospel, do you present the truth *clearly*?

To Pray

Ask God for an opportunity this week to share Christ's words on the cross—"It is finished!"—with a lost person. Ask for the words to clearly communicate this wonderful message.

Day 22

Who Is Your Real Employer?

To Read

> *Bondservants, obey in all things your masters according*
> *to the flesh, not with eyeservice, as men-pleasers, but in*
> *sincerity of heart, fearing God. And whatever you do,*
> *do it heartily, as to the Lord and not to men.*
>
> —Colossians 3:22–23

To Consider

You know who signs your paycheck. You know who does your performance evaluation. You also know who has the final word in authorizing a raise.

The question is, "Who is your *real* employer?" As you report to work every day, who do you actually work for?

Paul the apostle left no doubt—we work for God! The "bondservants" he spoke of were not employees but slaves. Instead of being salaried workers, they were the actual property of their masters. However, Paul's words apply to all servants and employees, whether in a household or in the world of industry, two thousand years ago or today.

Paul encourages us to "obey in all things your masters." As we labor, our work should be done from the heart, not merely from the head. We are to be God-pleasers, not people-pleasers. Slaves were tempted to please the master only when his eye was on them. Sound familiar? Christian slaves are exhorted by Paul to please the one whose eyes see everything. Ultimately, we are working for the Lord, not for our earthly boss.

"Fearing God" does not mean that we should be frightened of God if we don't perform perfectly. Instead, Paul is explaining that we are to stand in awe of who He is and of His authority over us. We owe a reverential respect to God because He is our ultimate employer. Our goal in all things is to please Him. Because of who He is and what He has done for us, we deeply desire to please Him, to do things that will honor Him and bring Him glory. Disobedience is never an option; only obedience will do.

When it comes to work, you need to be honest in all your dealings, because ultimately it's God to whom you answer. You don't come to work at 8:15 if you're supposed to be there at 8:00. You work just as hard five minutes before it is time to leave as you did in the middle of the morning. Your performance is the same when your employer's back is turned as when he or she is facing you. You are not concerned merely about whether or not your work meets the company's standards; you also want it to measure up to God's standards.

Your employer is God above, not a boss below. Keeping this in mind will never cause a non-Christian employer to say, "My non-Christian employees are better workers than my Christian ones." Hard, honest work will reflect your devotion to Jesus Christ in a real, tangible way.

To Illustrate

Mrs. Mamie Eisenhower, wife of President Dwight D. Eisenhower, used to say that the best words she heard her husband say at night were, "God, I did the best I could today." Then the late General Eisenhower would fall asleep.

As Christians, we ought to come to the end of each day, look up toward our Employer and say, "God, I did the best I could for You today."

To Meditate

Meditate on the fact that your obedience is due to the One who created both you and your employer.

To Pray

As you drive to work each day, or if driving is your work, pray this simple prayer: "Lord, help me to please You rather than people. May everything I do be sincere, because I'm working for You."

Day 23

Surviving Temptation

To Read

No temptation has overtaken you except such as is common to man; but God is faithful, who will not allow you to be tempted beyond what you are able, but with the temptation will also make the way of escape, that you may be able to bear it.

—1 Corinthians 10:13

To Consider

You will face temptation—guaranteed. Satan will make sure of it. And there is no lack of temptation in the workplace.

During a week you are struggling in your marriage, Satan will present the "ideal" mate—the coworker who understands you "like no one else can." As you travel, the person next to you on the plane may appear more compatible than your mate. Because you are away from home, who will ever know?

When finances are tight, Satan will have the funds available somewhere. And although the means are dishonest, he'll convince you, "It's just this one time. The boss will never find out." If the company reimburses you for mileage or expenses related to business, Satan will try to convince you that altering the numbers will help you quite a bit toward the purchase of your next vehicle. After all, that's something a lot of employees do.

The apostle Paul assured the Corinthian believers that the temptations they were experiencing were not unusual; they were "common to man." He assured them that God had not left them as victims of their circumstances. With *every* temptation, He will provide a way of escape. We serve a God who is faithful; He is dependable and trustworthy. *It's our responsibility to take the way of escape instead of succumbing to the temptation. As believers, we can be the victors, not the victims.*

Sometimes our best way of escape may be asking God for the strength to say "no." For example, if you're tempted by the thought of Internet pornography, He'll give you the strength to avoid lewd websites. Sometimes your way of escape will be to overcome wrong with good. Responding to harsh words from a mate with a thoughtful gift is a way of saying, "Let's forgive each other and move forward." Other times, the best way of escape may be to have a friend hold you accountable. A trusted friend, who is asked to oversee your expense reports or even your Internet activity, can encourage honesty.

To Illustrate

Have you ever watched bighorn sheep in the high mountains? Tourists can approach them from below and even take photos. But approach them from above, and the herd scatters. Why? They know that "the above" is their escape route. A mountain lion can come at them on level ground and easily overtake them. But when the bighorn climbs a slope full of boulders, it escapes every time. Its escape comes from looking upward.

Our escape from temptation also comes when we look upward. As we do, God shows us how to master temptation before it masters us.

To Meditate

When faced with temptation, where do you focus first: on the temptation or upward to the One who wants to show you the way out?

To Pray

Take a sheet of paper and list several things Satan could use to tempt you in your particular workplace. Plan ahead—just like children do in school when they practice a fire drill. Then ask God to help you consistently take the escape instead of falling into temptation.

Day 24

False Expectations

To Read

And you He made alive, who were dead in trespasses and sins, in which you once walked according to the course of this world, according to the prince of the power of the air, the spirit who now works in the sons of disobedience.
—Ephesians 2:1–2

To Consider

The boss's vocabulary seems to be limited to four-letter words. An employee feels like the whole world revolves around him and gets frustrated when it doesn't. A fellow engineer is your best friend one moment and worst enemy the next. The teachers' lounge is filled with gossipers intent on sticking their noses in everyone's business. The breath of a supervisor makes it clear his drinking controls him, not vice-versa. Another stay-at-home mom only wants to talk about her family, never about yours. A client doesn't seem to understand why you cannot drop everything to handle her problem immediately.

Questions fill your mind. Why can't they see what they are doing? Couldn't they give just one day a week to thinking about someone other than themselves? Why are they so bent on self-destruction?

Paul explained why in the second chapter of his letter to the Ephesians. Conduct like this originates in our fallen, sinful nature. Non-Christians do what non-Christians do for good reasons. First, they are spiritually "dead in trespasses and sins." They cannot understand or respond to spiritual things unless the Holy Spirit moves in their lives. As a person who is physically dead has no knowledge of his surroundings, a person who is spiritually dead cannot even see his needs.

Second, they walk "according to the course of this world." They have no moral standards, or the ones they have are wrong. Third, they are governed by "the prince of the power of the air, the spirit who now works in the sons of disobedience." They are followers of Satan instead of followers of God, so disobedience characterizes their lives. They act the way they do because they know nothing else. They are without Christ, dead in sin, godless in standards, and controlled by Satan. What more could we expect?

But we have been *set free*. Christ said, "Therefore if the Son makes you free, you shall be free indeed" (John 8:36).

Recognizing the lost condition of others should make our hearts bleed for them instead of becoming upset or frustrated with them. You may be the one God wants to use to show them the difference in a life controlled by Christ instead of by Satan.

To Illustrate

Leadership Journal reported the story of a Los Angeles County parking control officer who came upon a brown Cadillac El Dorado that was illegally parked next to the curb on a street-cleaning day. Ignoring the man slumped against the wheel as though he were sleeping, the officer reached inside the car window and placed a $30 citation on the dash. The driver never responded. He couldn't. Hours earlier he had been shot to death, and the officer didn't look closely enough to notice.

The lost around you at work are spiritually dead. Let's be keenly aware that they don't need a citation, they need a Savior.

To Meditate

When you see non-Christians doing what they do, do you roll your eyes in annoyance, or do you remember that without Jesus you would be doing the same sinful things?

To Pray

Ask God to help you look behind the person's actions to the real problem—spiritual death. Ask Him to help you respond with grace and kindness rather than a judgmental attitude.

Day 25

Enduring Persecution

To Read

> *If you are reproached for the name of Christ, blessed are you, for the Spirit of glory and of God rests upon you. On their part He is blasphemed, but on your part He is glorified. But let none of you suffer as a murderer, a thief, an evildoer, or as a busybody in other people's matters. Yet if anyone suffers as a Christian, let him not be ashamed, but let him glorify God in this matter.*
> —1 Peter 4:14–16

To Consider

Jesus Christ never said that the Christian life would be a popular or easy one. Much of what you say and do goes against the norm—especially in the workplace. The workplace sometimes says, "Watch out for number one." Christ says, "Put others first." The workplace says, "Get even; settle the score." Christ says, "Return good for evil." The workplace says, "Success is measured by money." God says, "Success is measured by faith." The workplace says, "You're here to have people serve you." God says, "You're here to serve others."

When we live out our faith, our lives become convicting to those around us. But instead of pointing the finger at themselves, others might point the finger at you.

Ridicule, frowns, exclusion from their parties, jokes that they deem funny but you don't, and conversations behind your back may become all too common.

Peter says that when you are reproached for the name of Christ, you have cause to rejoice. "Reproached" can also be translated as "insulted" or "ridiculed openly or secretly." But when you are ridiculed, God is glorified. Why? Because "the Spirit of glory and of God rests upon you." The insults and ridicule are a sign that others see the reflection of His glory in you. The good in you bothers them, and that's cause for celebration.

An old adage applies well here: "People only throw stones at trees that bear fruit." Every time people recognize you for your association with Jesus Christ and you suffer ridicule for it, you *are* blessed.

Peter further emphasizes his point by saying that when we suffer for doing things a Christian should not do, we have reason to be ashamed. Christians should not be murderers, thieves, evildoers, or busybodies in other people's lives. But if we suffer for the sake of our faith, we should rejoice!

To Illustrate

In his book *The Root of the Righteous*, A. W. Tozer wrote these fitting words: "A real Christian is an odd number anyway. He feels supreme love for One whom he has never seen, he talks familiarly every day to Someone he cannot see, expects to go to heaven on the virtue of Another, empties himself in order that he might be full, admits he is wrong so he can be declared right, goes down in order to get up, is strongest when he is weakest, richest when he is poorest, and happiest when he feels worst. He dies so he can live, forsakes in order to have, gives away so he can keep, sees the invisible, hears the inaudible, and knows that which passeth knowledge."

To Meditate

Think about any suffering or persecution you have experienced from your coworkers for your stand as a Christian. As you think of each incident, instead of saying, "Why, God?" say, "Thank you, God."

To Pray

Ask God to consistently draw attention to Himself through your life at work, so that even if you suffer, He will be glorified.

Day 26

Modeling Christ's Forgiveness

To Read

> *[Bear] with one another, and [forgive] one another, if anyone has a complaint against another; even as Christ forgave you, so you also must do.*
>
> —Colossians 3:13

To Consider

Someone wrongs you. You know how you'd *like* to respond. But which of the following represents the proper Christlike response?

- I'll forgive her, but I can't forget.
- I'll forgive him, but I'll bet you he does it again.
- I'll forgive her, but I want to see that there has been a change in her life.

The answer is obvious to anyone who has read the verse above. None of them represents a Christlike attitude.

Colossians 3:13 leaves no room for misunderstanding. When someone does something that hurts us, we are to bear with them. It does not say to "be a bear with them," growling and fighting back. Instead, it says we are to *bear with them*. We are to extend forgiveness without limits.

It continues, "If anyone has a complaint against another; even as Christ forgave you, so you also must do." Notice that it does not say that we have to forgive *because* Christ forgave us, although that is inherent in the thought. The idea is even bigger than that—"even *as* Christ forgave you." We need to forgive fully and completely, no strings attached.

Here's a great truth: When Christ forgives our sins, He throws them into a sea, and then He puts up a "No Fishing" sign. No one, not even Satan himself, can bring those sins to the surface again. That depth of pardon, that eagerness to put sin so far behind us, is the kind of forgiveness we are to extend in the workplace.

A fellow worker insults you; another one ridicules your heavenly Father. Your boss denies you the credit you deserve while giving your supervisor credit he does not deserve. A manager misrepresents you behind your back. Someone steals the tip left for you in the restaurant. You're misunderstood by those who are amazed that you don't party with them. A stay-at-home mother whose child you watched while she ran errands won't return the same favor. Jesus calls us to forgive. Does your forgiveness model His?

To Illustrate

Imagine God owning a computer that contains a list of all your wrongs. As you scroll through the list, not one has been overlooked. They are all there. In fact, some wrongs are repeatedly mentioned. Acts of unkindness, selfishness, hatred, and stealing have been typed in again and again. What happens when God forgives? He presses the delete button. Every sin is gone.

Are you as quick to press the delete button when others hurt you?

To Meditate

If someone wanted to know what Christ's forgiveness was like, would your forgiveness of others be a good picture?

To Pray

Ask God to help you to be as consistently quick and complete in your forgiveness of others as Christ is to forgive you.

Day 27

Not So Fast

To Read

> *Come now, you who say, "Today or tomorrow we will go to such and such a city, spend a year there, buy and sell, and make a profit"; whereas you do not know what will happen tomorrow. For what is your life? It is even a vapor that appears for a little time and then vanishes away. Instead you ought to say, "If the Lord wills, we shall live and do this or that."*

—James 4:13–15

To Consider

Bragging is never healthy.

Some believers in James's day were making a tragic mistake. As the Roman Empire developed, itinerant merchants would travel from one city to another, trading oil, grain, lumber, clothing, spices, fruits, gold, or precious stones. However, a serious problem had developed. Believers were conducting business as though God did not exist and they were the masters of their own destiny.

"Today or tomorrow" also can be translated as "today *and* tomorrow." The group James was addressing had decided that they would take a two-day journey. "We will go to such and such a city": they probably pointed to it on a map. "Spend a year there": the start and stop dates had been decided. "Buy and sell, and make a profit": they felt sure of a positive outcome.

James firmly addressed the problem, calling them on their plans. They did not take God's will for their lives into account. He warned, "For what is your life? It is even a vapor that appears for a little time and then vanishes away." We are not pillars made out of concrete; we are people made out of clay. As steam that comes up from a pot is seen one moment and is gone the next, we are not promised tomorrow. Therefore we must approach life with the attitude, "If the Lord wills, we shall live and do this or that." Each day, we must recognize that we are dependent upon Him for life itself. Our planning must never leave God out. Instead, we must place God first.

How will that type of thinking influence our conduct in the workplace? First, we recognize that each day is a gift from God for us to use wisely. Second, we want to be the best witness for Christ *today*, knowing that we are not promised a tomorrow. Third, our planning should always keep God in the center of our lives rather than at the circumference. All the plans we make are ultimately at His disposal.

To Illustrate

USA Today covered the memorial service for University of Arizona center Shawntinice Polk. A three-time all–Pac-10 basketball player, she collapsed at the school's arena and died during a practice. The medical examiner discovered a pulmonary blood clot, which is a rare occurrence for a healthy, twenty-two-year-old woman.

She had no idea when she woke up that morning that this would be her last day.

We can plan for tomorrow, but we cannot count on it.

To Meditate

As you plan everything from vacation to vocation, is your attitude, "If the Lord wills, I will . . . "?

To Pray

Ask God to help you enter the workplace each morning, mindful that you may not be there the next day. Ask Him to help you approach today with the realization that it's His gift for you to use wisely.

Day 28

Don't Worry About Others

To Read

Then Peter, turning around, saw the disciple whom Jesus loved following, who also had leaned on His breast at the supper, and said, "Lord, who is the one who betrays You?" Peter, seeing him, said to Jesus, "But Lord, what about this man?"

Jesus said to him, "If I will that he remain till I come, what is that to you? You follow Me."

—John 21:20–22

To Consider

How many times have you thought of Jesus as someone who tells you *not* to be concerned about others? It seems backward, doesn't it? On one occasion, though, that's exactly what He did.

Jesus had just informed Peter that he would one day suffer an agonizing death for his faith, outstretched on a cross (John 21:18). In the meantime, prior to his death, which would glorify God, Christ said to Peter, "Follow Me" (v. 19).

Peter looked back to see John—the disciple whom Jesus loved—following behind. Peter wanted to know what the future held for John. He asked, "What about this man?" (v. 21). In essence, he was saying, "You've told me what your will is for my life. What is your will for John's life?"

Had you been there, you probably would have been shocked by Christ's response, "If I will that he remain till I come, what is that to you?" His point was that God's will for John's life was none of Peter's business. Jesus focused Peter back on what He just told him to do: "You follow Me."

In the workplace, we are constantly tempted to focus on others. Those three words, "What about them?" are often foremost in our minds. Our intentions may be good. Peter may have wondered if the "fate" that ultimately would overtake him also would befall John. We may wonder if other believers understand the importance of following Jesus.

However, we also may be concerned out of a selfish or impure motive. Perhaps we are comparing our success to that of others. Ultimately, we must remember that when it comes to discipleship, two words matter most: "Follow Me." Don't concern yourself with unnecessary questions. Just follow Him.

To Illustrate

A national pastor who was later martyred for his faith in Zimbabwe said, "The die has been cast. I have stepped over the line. The decision has been made—I'm a disciple of His. I can't look back, let up, slow down, back away, or be still. My past is redeemed, my present makes sense, and my future is secure. I don't have to be right, first, tops, recognized, praised, regarded, or rewarded."

That is what it means to be a disciple of Jesus.

To Meditate

Are you asking God unnecessary questions or focusing on His will for other people rather than on your relationship with Him? Have you forgotten His simple words, "You follow Me"?

To Pray

Ask God to make one thing characterize your life— your desire to follow Jesus.

Day 29

You're Amazing

To Read

> *Pharaoh said to his servants, "Can we find such a one as this, a man in whom is the Spirit of God?"*
>
> *Then Pharaoh said to Joseph, "Inasmuch as God has shown you all this, there is no one as discerning and wise as you. You shall be over my house, and all my people shall be ruled according to your word; only in regard to the throne will I be greater than you."*
>
> —Genesis 41:38–40

To Consider

The most powerful way to encourage people to be amazed by God is by letting them be amazed at you.

Joseph is a case in point; check out his life and character as it unfolds in Genesis 39 and 40. He was a faithful laborer in difficult circumstances. He resisted temptation so that his master's godless mistress could not seduce him. He conducted himself with integrity as a keeper of the prison, and he won the favor of his supervisor. He did not seek revenge when confronted with false accusations and unjust punishment. Sudden prosperity did not trip him up. He walked through each day in dependence on God.

Note Pharaoh's words, "Can we find such a one as this?" Pharaoh acknowledged Joseph as exceptionally wise. God's power flowed through Joseph's life. Pharaoh was so impressed with Joseph that he made him ruler over all of Egypt. He was given such authority that only Pharaoh was above him.

You don't need the particular talents or giftedness of a Joseph. But could those who watch you in the workplace say, as they are positively impressed, "Can we find such a one as this?"

Perhaps they are referring to your integrity or dependability. They may be referring to your good work ethic or to the quality of what you do and the spirit with which it's done. Your positive attitude in the face of difficulty may impress them. Your coworkers might be influenced by the way you handle adverse circumstances or irritable people. Others could observe you and say, "You are amazing." You can build a platform for them to be amazed with Him.

To Illustrate

Christian Clippings carried the story of a woman who came to Christ and attributed her conversion to one of her employees. She explained, "She is just a poor obscure washerwoman who has served in my home for many years. I have never known her to be impatient, to speak an unkind word, or to do a dishonorable deed. I know of countless little acts of unselfish love that adorn her life. Shamefacedly, let me say that I have openly sneered at her faith and laughed at her fidelity to God. Yet when my little girl was taken away, it was this woman who caused me to look beyond the grave and shed my first tear of hope. The sweet magnetism of her life led me to Christ. I covet the thing that makes her life beautiful."

Amazed at the washerwoman, she became amazed by Him.

To Meditate

What are three areas of your life at work that could cause your coworkers to say, "Can we find such a one as this?"

To Pray

Ask God to make you the kind of worker that amazes people in such a way that they become amazed by Christ.

Day 30

How Do You See Lost People?

To Read

> *Then Jesus went about all the cities and villages, teaching in their synagogues, preaching the gospel of the kingdom, and healing every sickness and every disease among the people. But when He saw the multitudes, He was moved with compassion for them, because they were weary and scattered, like sheep having no shepherd.*
> —Matthew 9:35–36

To Consider

You watch your coworker sit down at the lunch table. You observe your boss working with a client. You see the manager clock in. You interact with the sales representative as you sign the contract. You greet the homeowner at the door as you prepare to examine her options for remodeling. You are about to talk to your patient about the lab results.

How do you view them? Are you looking at them through God's eyes?

Christ saw lost people with great sorrow, as sheep without a shepherd. Isn't it interesting that He compared us in our lost condition to sheep—not deer, horses, cats, or dogs? Pardon the frankness, but sheep are dumb and foolish; they are so prone to go astray.

Sheep will wander over to the edge of a cliff, even though a slip of one foot could send them quickly over the edge. They will leave the security of the shepherd for the insecurity of darkness or deep ravines. Even when they find a plush plot of grass, they will look for a hole in the fence so that they can feed on the inferior grass outside. They will wander over to a bush without realizing that underneath it lies a deadly snake. Stubborn. Foolish. Self-willed. Lacking direction. That's what sheep are like.

The biblical text does not say that Christ dreaded or despised them. "Compassion" suggests strong emotion. He felt deep sympathy for them. Such sympathy moved Jesus to ask the disciples to share the gospel and gather in those who trust in Him.

Do you view those you work with the same way He did? Do you respond in such a way that it is obvious you feel compassion for them? They are sheep without a shepherd. They need to know the One you know. Until they do, they will continue to wander in the wrong direction, doing the foolish things sheep do.

To Illustrate

Our Daily Bread told of a man who sold newspapers and shined shoes sixty years ago on the streets of downtown Boise, Idaho. He spoke of life in those days, life today, and how things have changed. When he was asked, "What's changed the most?" he answered, "People—they don't care anymore." As an example, he told of his mother who often fed hungry people who came to their house. Each day she prepared food for her family and then made meals for travelers in need. Once she asked a man how he happened to find her door. The man replied, "Your address is written on all the boxcar walls."

To Meditate

When you interact with non-Christians, do you think of them as lost sheep? Are you moved with compassion for them, as Jesus was?

To Pray

Ask God to help you see lost people the way He sees them. Whenever necessary, ask Him to change your heart into a heart of compassion.

Day 31

Faithful or Fruitful

To Read

> *Do you not say, "There are still four months and then comes the harvest"? Behold, I say to you, lift up your eyes and look at the fields, for they are already white for harvest! And he who reaps receives wages, and gathers fruit for eternal life, that both he who sows and he who reaps may rejoice together. For in this the saying is true: "One sows and another reaps." I sent you to reap that for which you have not labored; others have labored, and you have entered into their labors.*

—John 4:35–38

To Consider

God wants to use you in the workplace in a very unique and special way. He wants to use you to populate heaven. But does that mean you have failed if a person doesn't come to Christ when you share the gospel with him or her?

According to John 4, Christ had been in Samaria for only two days. He hadn't done any miracles, which would have authenticated the fact that He was God. Yet He stressed to the disciples how ripe Samaria was for a spiritual harvest. Back then, farmers knew that four months normally elapsed between the end of planting and the beginning of harvest.

Using that analogy Christ said, "Do you not say, 'There are still four months and then comes the harvest'? Behold, I say to you, lift up your eyes and look at the fields, for they are already white for harvest!" (Note that the existing spiritual ripeness Jesus referred to probably was due to the ministry of the Old Testament prophets or to the ministry of John the Baptist.) The disciples were about to reap spiritual fruit where others had sown.

Don't miss Christ's point: "And he who reaps receives wages, and gathers fruit for eternal life, that both he who sows and he who reaps may rejoice together." Both have their reward—the one who first shared the gospel and the one who actually saw the person trust Christ.

Your job is to bring Christ to the workplace. God's job is to bring those in the workplace to Christ. With some non-Christians, you will be the fourth of fifteen people God is going to use to bring the person to Christ. With another, you may be the fifth of twenty-five, and with still another, the third of ten. Enjoy the excitement when you are the eighth of eight!

Accept the "pressure" of presenting the gospel clearly as God gives you opportunity. But don't take pressure on your shoulders that God never intended for you to carry. Do your part; let God do His. You are responsible to be faithful; God is responsible for the resulting fruit.

To Illustrate

A believer witnessed to a lost friend about Christ. The lost person did not trust the Savior at that time, but he accepted the friend's invitation to join him two weeks later